A TRINITARIAN PRIMER

I dedicate this work to
Caitlin Grace Alexander and
Mary Elizabeth Ormerod,
our first grandchildren,
and constant reminders that God is love.

Feast of the Holy Trinity, May 30, 2010

A TRINITARIAN PRIMER

Neil Ormerod

LITURGICAL PRESS
Collegeville, Minnesota

www.litpress.org

'Nihil Obstat: Reverend Robert Harren, *Censor deputatus*.

Imprimatur: ✠ Most Reverend John F. Kinney, J.C.D., D.D.,
                 Bishop of Saint Cloud, Minnesota,
                 August 2, 2010.

The Nihil Obstat and Imprimatur are a declaration that a book or
pamphlet is considered to be free from doctrinal or moral error. It
is not necessarily implied that those who have granted them agree
with the contents, opinions or statements expressed.'

The Scripture quotations in this book are from the New Revised
Standard Version of the Bible ©1989 by the Division of Christian
Education of the National Council of the Churches of Christ in
the United States of America. Used with permission. All rights
reserved.

First published in 2010 by St Pauls Publications, Australia

North American edition published in 2011 by
The Liturgical Press, Collegeville, Minnesota.
www.litpress.org
ISBN 978-0-8146-3355-7

Australian edition published by
ST PAULS PUBLICATIONS
35 Meredith St – PO Box 906
Strathfield NSW 2135
http://www.stpauls.com.au
ISBN 978 1 921472 67 1

A National Library of Australia Cataloguing-in-Publication entry
is available for this book.

Dewey Number: 231.044

Cover design by Kylie Prats
Cover image © Dreamstime.com / Maxim Sokolov

Printed in China by Everbest

Contents

Preface

Over the years I often have taught courses on the Trinity to theological students which have always been well received. I have also published academic articles and a book on the Trinity designed for a scholarly readership. However, this is the first time I have ventured into a more accessible account of trinitarian belief.

As with many things the origins of this book are a matter of happenchance. One evening I was at an Iftar dinner (when Muslims break their daily Ramadan fast) where I was sitting next to a young Muslim man. He talked about how his mother's side of the family was all Catholic and his father's side was all Muslim, so when he was a youth he set out on a spiritual journey to try to determine where his religious future lay. The one thing he could not get his head around in relation to Christianity was the doctrine of the Trinity. He said he even spoke to a bishop but no light was shed on the topic for him.

That setting was not the time or place to engage in a spirited defense of Christian trinitarian belief, but it did highlight a problem. The very next day

I had been invited to take a class at a Pentecostal theological college on Augustine's theology of the Trinity. The class went well and helped the students appreciate Augustine's profound contribution. At the end of the class one of the students asked, "Where can I read about this?" I knew my more academic pieces were available for that purpose but, given the previous night's encounter, I knew too there was a need for a more accessible work which spelt out the nature of Christian and Catholic belief than my more academic writings. Hence this present work.

Belief in the Trinity is one of Christianity's more difficult aspects for many people to understand and this is often reflected by the low level of homilies on Trinity Sunday. The situation has been eased by the resurgence in trinitarian theology in the past decades, but I am not convinced that current trends in trinitarian theology are as helpful as the more traditional directions taken by greats such as Augustine and Aquinas. The problem is getting their insights into a more palatable form. And so I have structured this work around three chapters. The first chapter considers the scriptural material on the Trinity and seeks to address the question, "From where does our trinitarian faith arise?" The second chapter looks at the trinitarian aspects of the Nicene Creed, the Creed we say every Sunday in the Mass. The purpose of the chapter is to elucidate what the Creed means and its implications for our belief. The third chapter asks the question, "How can we understand the Trinity?" as an exercise in "faith seeking understanding," the classical definition of theology given by St Anselm. And so it considers analogy as a way of furthering our understanding, in particular, the central analogy offered by Augustine in his writing on the Trinity.

I have also included three appendixes dealing with specific matters. The first is the controversial matter of gender and the Trinity. It seeks to address concerns raised by some of the "maleness" of trinitarian language. The second appendix consists of some homily notes for those seeking to preach on the Trinity, using the three sets of readings provided in the Catholic Lectionary for Trinity Sunday. I hope these notes prove useful. The third appendix is a glossary of terms used in relation to trinitarian belief.

I would like to thank the publishers, The Liturgical Press (USA) and St Pauls Publications (Australia), for their interest and support of this project, and their helpful suggestions in finalizing the text. I would also like to thank my colleague Dr Clare Johnson and some of her students who "trialed" the first draft of the text. Finally I would like to thank Christopher Brennan for his meticulous editing of the text.

CHAPTER 1

The Trinity
and the Scriptures

Any account of the Trinity must begin with the Scriptures. Having said this, however, there are some difficulties associated with the use of the Scriptures in attempting to ground an account of the Trinity. We want to be able to say that our faith is grounded in the Scriptures, but at the same time we must acknowledge that the precise expression that we find in later councils and theologians is the product of hundreds of years of discussion and debate. We need to affirm the primacy of the scriptural witness, but not neglect the contribution of the believing community as the privileged place for reading the Scriptures.

Over the past sixty years or so, Catholics have learnt to approach the Scriptures in a very different way from before. We have been encouraged to read the scriptural text according to its "literary form," that is, to attend to the particular type of literature each book, and each part of each book, of the Bible is. And so we might read the letters

of Paul in a different way from the Gospels, and
the Gospels in a different way from the Psalms.
Different literature requires different sensitivities
be employed for it to be fully appreciated and
properly understood. Also we have been asked
to attend to the "intention of the author," that is,
to seek to understand the text as a product of a
particular time and place, a history and culture.
The end result of this new approach is that it is
more difficult to simply quote the Bible as a source
of "proof texts" for various teachings and beliefs.
Such practices that were common in the past in
setting out Christian beliefs are not as acceptable
today as they once were. And so our approach to
Scripture might seem more roundabout to some,
but it is more in keeping with contemporary
readings of Scripture.

The Old Testament and the Trinity

We shall now turn our attention to the Old
Testament and its relationship to trinitarian
belief. Our intention is not to claim that the Old
Testament provides evidence of belief in or a
revelation of the Trinity. However, it is clear that
the authors of the New Testament used the Old
Testament as a resource in coming to grips with the
unique and definitive events surrounding Jesus –
his life, death, resurrection and the sending of his
Spirit. We shall now consider some of the resources

that they utilized from the Old Testament in their explication of these new events.

The Spirit of God

Some Old Testament texts refer to the spirit of God in relationship to: prophecy (e.g., Judg 14:6); the Messiah (Isa 61:1 – "The spirit of the Lord GOD is upon me") or creation (cf. Gen 2:7 where the Lord GOD breathes life into the human being); or they simply express the closeness of God to his people (Ps 139:7 – "Where can I go from your spirit?"). The spirit is also linked to the initial act of creation (Gen 1:2 – "a wind from God swept over the face of the waters", where we note that the Hebrew word for "wind" is the same as that for "spirit").

The question which confronts these texts is whether God's spirit is thought of as:

- personal, that is, a distinct personal being;
- a personification of the divine closeness, that is, a literary device to express the closeness of God to the chosen people; or
- simply an impersonal divine force?

The variety of texts and contexts does not admit of a simple answer. The Old Testament was not interested in such speculation as to the metaphysical features of the spirit. It was interested in the way in which God's presence was manifest among the chosen people through the power of the divine spirit.

Nonetheless there are distinct elements of continuity between Old Testament references to the spirit and the New Testament conception of the Holy Spirit. The New Testament writers did not see themselves as introducing a new character into the drama of salvation, but rather as giving a more solid identity to one already known, so that the spirit present in the history of Israel is none other than the Spirit of Jesus that they experienced at Pentecost.

Divine Wisdom

In the trinitarian debates of the early church, one of the most quoted verses was Proverbs 8:22, "The LORD created me [Wisdom] at the beginning of his work, the first of his acts of long ago." The reference to Wisdom was taken to mean the same as John 1:1 which talks of God's Word, and seemed to imply that the Word/Wisdom was a creature. Today this seems wrong-headed because it is difficult to think of the "intention of the author" as including a trinitarian meaning to this text. More generally, Old Testament Wisdom literature portrays Wisdom as a semi-divine figure:

> There is in her a spirit that is intelligent, holy,
> unique, manifold, subtle,
> mobile, clear, unpolluted,
> distinct, invulnerable, loving the good, keen,
> irresistible, beneficent, humane,

> steadfast, sure, free from anxiety,
> all-powerful, overseeing all,
> and penetrating through all . . .
> For she is a breath of the power of God,
> and a pure emanation of the glory of the
>   Almighty. (Wis 7:22-26)

It is clear that we are dealing with a person-ification of a divine attribute here. Is this person-ification simply a literary device, a metaphor for speaking of God's wisdom in more personal terms? Or does the author intend us to read this as implying that Wisdom is a distinct, real being? Clearly we are dealing with an extended theological interest in the notion of divine wisdom. But is this anything more than a way of praising God in an indirect manner?

What is clear is that the New Testament authors found in the Wisdom writings a powerful source for their reflections on the Person of Jesus. The repeated references to "through him all things came into being" – John 1:3; 1 Corinthians 8:6; Colossians 1:15-20; Hebrews 1:2-3 – are all direct references to the creative role of Wisdom identified in the Old Testament.

The Divine Word

Though it seems to more directly relate to the New Testament theme of the Word, or Logos (John 1:1), in fact the Old Testament theme of the divine word is relatively minor, arising mainly in the prophetic tradition. The classical text is Isaiah 55:10-11:

> For as the rain and the snow come down from heaven,
> and do not return there until they have watered the earth,
> making it bring forth and sprout,
> giving seed to the sower and bread to the eater,
> so shall my word be that goes out from my mouth;
> it shall not return to me empty,
> but it shall accomplish that which I purpose,
> and succeed in the thing for which I sent it.

The word is also the divine instrument at creation, for example in Psalm 33:6-9:

> By the word of the LORD the heavens were made,
> and all their host by the breath of his mouth.
> He gathered the waters of the sea as in a bottle;
> he put the deeps in storehouses.
>
> Let all the earth fear the LORD;
> let all the inhabitants of the world stand in awe of him.
> For he spoke, and it came to be;
> he commanded, and it stood firm.

Clearly this echoes the Genesis account wherein creation is the product of God's word. However there is little evidence that this word is personified in the way divine wisdom is.

The Divine Name

Another element which becomes a resource for New Testament writers is the notion of the divine name, YHWH. This name is revealed in the classic Exodus text, Exodus 3:14, where YHWH gives his name to Moses as "I AM WHO I AM." In ancient cultures the "name" of a person was viewed as somehow representing the person, or as manifesting the person's power. In certain Old Testament texts, for example Deuteronomy 12:5 and 12:11, the name appears as an extension of the person, a distinct, almost personified being:

> But you shall seek the place that the LORD your God will choose out of all your tribes as his habitation to put his name there. You shall go there . . . then you shall bring everything that I command you to the place that the LORD your God will choose as a dwelling for his name: your burnt offerings and your sacrifices, your tithes and your donations, and all your choice votive gifts that you vow to the LORD.

The Gospel of John in particular seems to identify Jesus with the divine name in the use of the phrase "I am" (John 8:58). Some early church fathers in fact identified Jesus with YHWH, the divine name revealed in the Old Testament.

One God

While there are these hints and a suggestion of "plurality" linked with divinity in the Old Testament, <u>the other outstanding feature of the Old Testament is its insistence upon the unity of God and its complete rejection of any suggestion of polytheism</u>, for example, Deuteronomy 6:45:

> Hear, O Israel: The LORD is our God, the LORD alone. You shall love the LORD your God with all your heart, and with all your soul, and with all your might.

It is this strict monotheism which will raise questions for the first generation of Christian thinkers: how will they reconcile their insights into the Persons of Jesus and the Spirit with the strict understanding of God as one?

We can see from this material in the Old Testament that there are constant attempts to bridge the gap between the transcendent God and the felt divine presence among the chosen people. All of the terms we have considered, Spirit, Word, Wisdom, Name, are attempts to express a closer relationship between God and the created order. These terms will become a natural resource for the writers of the New Testament when they come to identify the unique closeness they experience in Jesus Christ and the outpouring of the Holy Spirit.

The Trinity and the New Testament

We have already seen that the Old Testament provided New Testament authors with a set of resources by which to speak of the new revelation they experienced in Jesus Christ. Two questions emerge:

1. What evidence do we have of this "newness" in the New Testament, that is, what evidence is there for a basic trinitarian belief in the New Testament?

2. What experiences led the New Testament authors to express their faith in this trinitarian manner?

We shall begin with the issue of the Person of God the Father.

God the Father

Perhaps most Christians fall into an easy identification of the God of the New Testament with the God of the Old Testament, and hence identify God the Father with the revelation of God active in the history of Israel. However we have already noted that the identification of God the Father (New Testament) with YHWH (Old Testament) was not uniform among early Christian writers. Some preferred to identify YHWH with the pre-existent Jesus. Some unorthodox groups sought to break the unity of the two testaments by opposing Old Testament and New Testament accounts of God, speaking of two gods revealed in the two testaments, one a creator god, the other a savior god.

What we see here is a struggle to express what is truly new in the New Testament in relation to the Old Testament. We are familiar with the notion of the divine fatherhood evident in the Old Testament narrative of the chosen people. The chosen people are the sons and daughters of God, who exercises a fatherly and providential care of his people. The king, in particular, is a Son of God, as found in the royal enthronement psalm, Psalm 2:7:

> I will tell of the decree of the LORD:
> He said to me, "You are my son;
> today I have begotten you.

Still, this image of fatherhood is one of several used of God in the Old Testament. God is also husband, as in Hosea; or a nursing mother, as in Isaiah 49:15:

> Can a woman forget her nursing child,
> or show no compassion for the child of her
>   womb?
> Even these may forget,
> yet I will not forget you.

In regard to the fatherhood of God, the cate-chetical text "God the Father of Mercy," published by the International Theological Commission, notes:

In the Old Testament, the title "Father" when
referring to God, expresses primarily God's
creative power, protection, authority, and
maintenance of life. It is a powerful allusion to
the goodness, at once fatherly and motherly,
that God as provident creator demonstrates vis-
à-vis the people in need.

Still, the revelation of the New Testament is more
than a revelation of the general fatherhood of
God. Rather it is a revelation of God the Father.
How is this different?

What we find in the New Testament is Jesus'
reference to God as Abba, Father (Mark 14:36),
which strikes a note of intimate relationship not
found in the Old Testament references. Further,
this relationship is specific to Jesus, one which we
are invited to share, but not one which is "natural"
to us. We become "adopted" sons and daughters of
the Father, whereas Jesus' relationship is defining
of his identity in some sense:

He destined us for adoption as his children
through Jesus Christ, according to the good
pleasure of his will. (Eph 1:5)

Our relationship to the Father is dependent upon
Jesus' relationship, which enjoys some type of
priority:

Jesus said to her [Mary Magdalene], "Do not
hold on to me, because I have not yet ascended
to the Father. But go to my brothers and say

to them, 'I am ascending to my Father and
your Father, to my God and your God.' " (John
20:17)

What emerges from this is the special relationship
that exists between Jesus and the one he calls
Father, a relationship he alone experiences in a
distinctive manner. This relationship is defining
not only of the personal identity of Jesus, but also
of the Person of God the Father. The distinctiveness
of God the Father is also given in this relationship.
Further, the experiential grounding of our belief
in God the Father is found precisely in the
relationship that Jesus experiences and speaks of
in his prayer, his sense of mission, his sense of
obedience, and his resurrection. Without this we
would know God as father (an attribute), but not
God the Father (a Person). In this sense we cannot
speak of God the Father without also raising the
question of God the Son, incarnate as the human
being Jesus of Nazareth.

God the Son

As we have seen in our discussion of God the
Father, the question of the Person of the Father
cannot be separated from discussion of the Person
of the Son. What specifies the distinctiveness
of the New Testament witness is precisely the
relationship between Father and Son:

> All things have been handed over to me by my
> Father; and no one knows the Son except the
> Father, and no one knows the Father except the
> Son and anyone to whom the Son chooses to
> reveal him. (Matt 11:27)

Still, the question can be asked: to what extent does the New Testament show belief in the divinity of Jesus?

While many would consider this a central belief to be found in the New Testament, a careful consideration of the New Testament material reveals two features:

1. Widespread material, across all New Testament authors, which suggests a "functional" divinity for Jesus; that is, Jesus is involved in activities, either during his life, or in his risen state, or at times in pre-existence, which are normally reserved to God, such as creation, forgiveness of sins, and judgment of sinners. We also see here the use of a plurality of titles drawn from the Old Testament indicating the special status of Jesus, titles such as "Son of Man," "Son of David," "Lord" and so on.

2. Given this widespread material there nonetheless remains a reticence to state explicitly the identification of Jesus with God. While there are some verses which are ambiguous as to their reference, there are really only a couple of direct texts: the well-known texts in John's Gospel: John

1:1: "In the beginning was the Word, and the Word was with God, and the Word was God"; and John 20:28, where Thomas proclaims to the risen Jesus, "My Lord and my God"; and perhaps Titus 2:13 ("the glory of our great God and Savior, Jesus Christ") and 2 Peter 1:1 ("the righteousness of our God and Savior Jesus Christ"), both of the last two depending upon whether one puts a comma before the "and" or not.

This observation reveals some of the tensions that the New Testament authors must have experienced in proclaiming "something new" while recognizing potential conflicts with existing Jewish monotheism; hence their reticence. It is precisely this ambiguity which will provide ample room for conflict over the next three hundred years leading up to the Councils of Nicaea and Constantinople.

Still, the question arises as to what experiences underpinned these beliefs in "something new" in the Person of Jesus? We have already considered the unique relationship which Jesus experienced with God the Father. Certainly this may ground a claim for Jesus' special status, but again we must ask how such a claim may be verified. It is difficult to avoid the conclusion that the verification of the claim is grounded in the disciples' experience of the risen Jesus. What is it that Jesus does in the resurrection that only God can do? What is it that the disciples experience that leads them to break all the rules they had learnt about how to speak of God? Certainly it must have been a powerful experience.

To answer this more fully requires attention to the third Person in our inquiry, the Holy Spirit, for, as Paul states: "no one can say 'Jesus is Lord' except by the Holy Spirit" (1 Cor 12:3). The interior transformation of the disciples by the Holy Spirit is a constitutive element in the proclamation of Jesus as Lord. Who or what then is this Holy Spirit?

God the Holy Spirit

When we turn our attention to the question of the Holy Spirit, we find a new set of problems. The first is the complete absence of any text which clearly identifies the Spirit as God. The reticence at speaking explicitly of the Son as God is here increased to the point of silence. This will cause problems in later debates in the early church. Most of the early debates concerned the divinity of the Son/Word/Logos; the Spirit is added as almost an afterthought, with some awareness that the problems associated with the biblical data make this a bold move.

The second problem concerns the continuity/ discontinuity between Old Testament and New Testament in relation to the Spirit. There is a certain sense in which the New Testament authors want to convey a sense of continuity between the two testaments. But as we saw earlier, there are questions about the "personhood" of the Spirit as represented in the Old Testament. At times the Spirit appears more as an impersonal force, a symbol of the divine presence in the world. In the New Testament however there are indications of the "personhood" of the Spirit, for example, in Paul's letters the Spirit is grieved (Rom 8:14), bears witness (Rom 8:16), cries (Rom 8:26), leads (Gal 4:6) and makes intercession (Eph 4:30). All these can be thought of as "personal" activities in a commonsense manner. On the other hand the New Testament also uses impersonal images of the Spirit, such as tongues of fire (Acts 2:2-3) and a dove (Mark 1:10), to convey the presence of the Spirit.

What is clearly new in the New Testament is the linking of the Spirit with the Person of Jesus. The Spirit is present in the very conception of Jesus (Luke 1:35); the Spirit drives Jesus into the wilderness (Mark 1:12); the Spirit rests on Jesus and remains with him (John 1:32); Jesus promises to send another Paraclete who will reveal the truth (John 16:12-15); and Jesus breathes forth the Spirit in his dying breath, and as his first act as risen Lord (John 20:22). At one time the connection is so close that Paul seems to identify the risen Jesus with the Spirit (2 Cor 3:16-18).

Further, the New Testament reveals the closeness of the Spirit to divinity in various ways. The Spirit is God's agent of revelation (2 Cor 2:9-11); the Spirit intercedes for us in prayer when we do not know how to pray (Rom 8:26-27); and the Spirit gifts the Christian community with a diversity of charisms through our baptism (1 Cor 12:4-13). All of these give the Spirit a special role in the economy of salvation, one closely linked with both the Father and Jesus. Despite this, however, we must conclude that teaching on the Holy Spirit in the New Testament remains underdeveloped, a fact which will impact on doctrinal development in later centuries.

The Triadic Formulas

A final though important factor in ongoing development of trinitarian belief has been the occurrence of the so-called "triadic" formulas within the New Testament. These are short, possibly creedal, statements which bring Father, Son and Spirit into conjunction in significant ways. They occur in various writings of the New Testament, particularly in the letters of Paul.

Perhaps the most famous is the trinitarian blessing of 2 Corinthians 13:13: "The grace of the Lord Jesus Christ, the love of God, and the communion of the Holy Spirit be with all of you." However, there are many other such triadic references, such as:

> But we must always give thanks to God for you, brothers and sisters beloved by the Lord, because God chose you as the first fruits for salvation through sanctification by the Spirit and through belief in the truth. For this purpose he called you through our proclamation of the good news, so that you may obtain the glory of our Lord Jesus Christ. (2 Thess 13-14)

> Now there are varieties of gifts, but the same Spirit; and there are varieties of services, but the same Lord [i.e., Jesus]; and there are varieties of activities, but it is the same God who activates all of them in everyone. (1 Cor 12:46)

> And because you are children, God has sent the Spirit of his Son into our hearts, crying, "Abba! Father!" (Gal 4:6)

> I appeal to you, brothers and sisters, by our Lord Jesus Christ and by the love of the Spirit, to join me in earnest prayer to God on my behalf. (Rom 15:30)

Most of these formulas operate within the economy of salvation ("for us and our salvation"), that is, they specify roles and activities which occur in the ongoing drama of human salvation. They spell out the trinitarian narrative of the Christian life, guided by the Spirit, in discipleship with Jesus, drawn towards the Father. <u>One formula however stands out as different from the rest, Matthew 28:19:</u> "Go therefore and make disciples of all nations, baptizing them in the name of the Father and of the Son and of the Holy Spirit." What makes this formula different is <u>the radical equality with which each Person is treated:</u> no distinct roles or activities are given; simply baptism in the three names.

Some suggest that this text is the most important witness to the Trinity in the New Testament because it provides concise expression of the basic trinitarian structure of Christian belief. Certainly the early church quickly adopted baptism in the three names, and included a threefold profession of faith as part of the baptismal vows. This liturgical practice will provide an undercurrent for later doctrinal debates.

Does the New Testament Provide Sufficient Grounding for Trinitarian Faith?

The question of the role of Scripture in determining our trinitarian faith is a constant issue in this field of study. There are several ways to address such a question.

The naïve approach, which is often used in catechesis, is to amass biblical texts which refer to Father, Son and Spirit and conclude that it is obviously the case that the New Testament evidence is sufficient to ground trinitarian faith. There are two major difficulties with this approach:

1. It ignores difficult questions which may arise in relation to any or all of the texts quoted. These questions highlight the tensions that may be present within the overall witness of the New Testament. These are not insurmountable but the difficulties need to be acknowledged.

2. It undercuts the interpretative role of the church itself in "reading" the text. The Scriptures are the book of the church and it must be read within the range of meanings provided by the church. And so it took the church centuries to formulate the more precise position found in its Creeds.

And so we note that in the doctrinal disputes of the next three centuries all the parties involved freely quoted the Scriptures. Each had their favorite texts by which they sought to "prove" their particular position. In the end the debates were not resolved simply by reference to the Scriptures but by reference to the practices of the church, its prayers and rituals, all of which reflected the trinitarian nature of Christian faith.

So we might accept that there has been a legitimate process of doctrinal development

which has taken the Scriptures as a starting point
and foundation. The nature of the process of such
development need not concern us here, but it is a
reminder that the Scriptures are to be read "with
the mind of the church" and not against it.

We may ask ourselves how the "mind of the
church" itself is formed, and we should note that
the ways in which the Scriptures are read in the
church are more than just ways of communicating
a truth to us. The Scriptures are the word of
God spoken to us; they are God's meaningful
communication to us, spoken through human
words and human authors. They speak to the
head, but not just the head, and so impact upon
us in various ways.

And so meaning has a *communicative*
function. The meaning grasped by one person is
communicated to another person through gesture,
art, symbols, words and through a life well lived.
Primarily Jesus communicates his own trinitarian
life to his disciples through his own prayer
(Abba, Father), his parables, his intimate sharing
of his own Spirit. Jesus talks about his Father
in heaven, about the Spirit that fills him, and
invites his followers to share in these with him.
Consequently his disciples continue this process
of communication through their gestures, art,
symbols, words and lives well lived, initiating us
all into the life of the Trinity. The written word of

the Scriptures plays a major but not exclusive role in this communication of trinitarian meaning.

Meaning also has an *identity-making* function, that is, it constitutes the identity of the Christian community. The language of the Scriptures identifies the community as a trinitarian community at its very core. We are members of the Body of Christ; Christ lives in us; Christ calls us his friends; we are sons and daughters in the one Son; we are temples of the Holy Spirit; the Spirit is poured into our hearts, and prays in the depths of them; we are adopted sons and daughters of the Father and coheirs of the kingdom; the Son goes to make a home for us in his Father's house. In these ways we can see that the Scriptures convey to the Christian community a sense of its trinitarian identity.

These two roles that meaning has continue to be expressed in the ways in which the trinitarian language of the Scriptures infiltrates our liturgies, hymns, prayers, art, etc. And so we might think not only of our Creed, but also of our baptismal rite, and the Gloria and Eucharistic Prayers at Mass. Meaning continues to shape our faith imaginations through the trinitarian symbols and narratives of the Scriptures. This is the continuing, lived experience of the church.

Meaning also has an *effective* function. It moves people to action and transforms their living. The Scriptures move us towards a life of mission. We are called to "go and make disciples, in the name of the Father, Son and Spirit." Just as the Father sends the Son, so we too are sent. We are sent or missioned by the Father to follow in the footsteps of the Son, empowered by his Spirit poured into our hearts. Transformed by the mission of the Son, we are called to live in significantly different ways, in ways which reflect the trinitarian glory of God. This is our sharing or participation in the life of the Trinity. Inasmuch as we share in the missions of the Son and the Spirit we share in God's own trinitarian life.

Finally meaning has a *cognitive* function, that is, the meaning expressed makes a claim to what really is, the truth, what is real, what is so. This role of meaning invites us to accept the meaning of Scripture as true, while not neglecting the fact that this truth is conveyed through a variety of means. As Christians we believe that the Scriptures reveal truth; however, as intelligent believers we appreciate the fact that the truth is not immediate in the text, but is mediated by the mode of expression appropriate to the type of literature used. This precludes the possibility of using Scripture as a source of proof texts for "proving" our arguments. On the other hand, to deny or exclude the truth of the meaning of the Scriptures would be to reduce the meaning to being merely metaphorical, without any significant truth claim at all.

We may also relate these four various functions of meaning to the traditional distinction between *fides qua*, the faith by which we believe, and *fides quae*, the faith which we believe. The cognitive meaning of the Scriptures relates directly, but not literally, to *the faith which we believe*. It is an expression in a religiously informed common sense of the meanings which will find more precise expression in the language of the church councils, particularly the Council of Nicaea, which we will consider in the next chapter. The effective, identity-making and communicative functions of meaning relate to *the faith by which we believe*. They are the faith-forming functions of meaning, the functions which shape our inner eye of faith, which transform our hearts and minds to be open to the true meanings present in the Scriptures. They are the functions of meaning which create the "mind of the church."

Conclusion

It is often the case that a consideration of the Scriptures leaves us with more questions than answers. The original trinitarian richness of the Scriptures will come up against hard questions about the claims made by Christian believers. Is Christianity tritheistic, that is, do we believe in three Gods? If the Father, Son and Spirit are God, why are there not three Gods? Or are they simply distinct manifestations of the one divine being, appearing as three for our sake, but not reflecting distinctions within God's own being? – a position known as modalism. Are the Son and the Spirit God in the same sense as the Father is God, or is there a real subordination between the Persons so that the Father is "more" God than the Son and the Spirit? – a position usually referred to as subordinationism. These are questions which were not within the scope of the authors of the New Testament. The answers to them would take some time in coming. However, given the nature of this short work we shall not look at the process by which these questions were answered. Instead, we will consider simply the endpoint of this process: the formal Creed of the Councils of Nicaea and Constantinople.

CHAPTER 2

The Creed of Nicaea:
Substance and Relations

While the Scriptures are perhaps our starting point for identifying where our belief in the Trinity comes from, it is perhaps not the first place in which Catholics encounter that belief. Rather that encounter is more likely to be liturgical. Indeed the whole of the eucharistic liturgy has a trinitarian resonance to it – the Gloria, the Creed, the Eucharistic Prayer and so on. All these prayers in one way or another speak to us of our Christian belief in the Trinity. More specifically we baptize in the name of the "Father, Son and Holy Spirit" and make the sign of the cross with the same trinitarian formula. Perhaps the most significant prayer, which historically has its origins in the great trinitarian debates of the fourth century, is the Creed, usually referred to as the Nicene Creed. This Creed was hammered out in two great church councils, one at Nicaea (325 AD) and one at Constantinople (381 AD). The central issue these councils sought to deal with was that of

the divinity of Jesus and to a lesser extent that of
the Spirit, beliefs which had been challenged by
followers of Arius, a priest from Alexandria.

I do not intend to go into the historical
details of these debates which are covered in
standard works on the topic. What I would
like to do is uncover the logic of the Creed in
its assertion of belief in the divinity of the Son
and Spirit in light of the theological accounts of
the early church fathers such as Athanasius, the
Cappadocian fathers (Basil and Gregory of Nyssa,
and Gregory Nazianzus) and Augustine. As such
it is a clarification of the logic of Nicaea through
a consideration of keys terms such as "substance,"
"procession" and "relation." We shall begin with
a statement of the key elements of the Creed.

The Nicene Creed

The Creed begins with the familiar affirmation of
belief in "God, the Father, the Almighty, maker of
heaven and earth, of all that is, seen and unseen."
We have already noted in the previous chapter
that we should not immediately identify "God
the Father" with the God spoken of in the Old
Testament. One can know God the Father only as
"the Father of our Lord and Savior Jesus Christ."
Here the Creed identifies a pre-eminent role in
creation with the Father; however this is not to say
that the Son and the Spirit are not involved also in

creation. The Creed will also say that "through him [i.e., the Son] all things were made" and identify the Spirit as "the Lord, the giver of life." So each of the Persons is involved in the act of creation, not just the Father. In the theology of Augustine (354–430 AD), largely followed in the West, the Father, Son and Spirit are equally creators of everything that exists. However because the Father is the source (but not creator) of the Son and the Spirit, it is not inappropriate to speak of the Father as creator in the way the Creed does.

However, this was not the main concern of those framing the Creed. Their main concern was the divinity of the Son. Challenged by Arius (d. 336 AD), the bishops of the council found it necessary to make as strong an affirmation as they could concerning the divinity of Jesus:

> We believe in one Lord, Jesus Christ,
> the only Son of God,
> eternally begotten of the Father,
> God from God, Light from Light,
> true God from true God,
> begotten, not made,
> one in Being with the Father.

It is worth taking each of these phrases in turn.

We believe in one Lord, Jesus Christ, the only Son of God

This is stated as an object of belief. It is not
something worked out purely on the basis of
human reasoning, but is something revealed to us
for an assent of faith. Jesus is "Lord," a term used
in the Old Testament to avoid uttering the name
of God. Yet he is not designated as God simply,
but as the "Son of God." It is this designation as
Son which raises questions. How can God have a
Son? How can we make distinctions within God?
For if we cannot make such distinctions, either
the Son is just another name for the Father, not a
distinct Person, or the Son is a creature. This was
the dilemma posed by Arius.

Eternally begotten of the Father . . . begotten, not made

Of course it was not the purpose of the council
to explain how we can make distinctions within
God; its task was to teach what the church
believes. With the phrases "eternally begotten"
and "begotten, not made," the council makes
a distinction between being made (i.e., being
a creature) and being "begotten." The term
"begotten" is of course from the Scriptures (John
1:14 – this does not come out in all translations

but it is in the original Greek). In its own way the term expresses a relationship, one with its origin in the Father, and its end point in the Son. The Father is the source of the being of the Son, but he is not the creator of the Son (the Son is "not made"). The relation of being "begotten" is like our human relationship of father and son, but it is also very different. It is "eternal," and so is always part of the divine existence. There is not a time when the Father is not Father of the Son; nor the Son, Son of the Father. There is also no sense of a divine "mother" involved in the process. The Father is the sole source of the Son. Here it is worth noting the mistaken biology of the ancient world which understood the father as the sole source of the new child; the male seed ("semen") was planted in the woman's womb which merely provided the "soil" for the seed to grow. So the term "Father" designates a sole source without a need for a divine mother.

God from God, Light from Light, true God from true God

Here the Creed uses the simple device of repetition to drive home its point. Both Father and Son are God, Light and true God. There is no room here for misunderstanding or compromise. Each of these phrases was added to ensure that the followers of

Arius had no way to wriggle around the teaching
that the council wanted to proclaim about Jesus.
Still, while each is equally God, these phrases also
imply an ordering, "God *from* God" and so on.
The Son is from the Father, begotten, not made.
The technical term used for this ordering in later
theology is "procession." The Son proceeds from
the Father. This is the general term that the Creed
will employ when speaking of the relation of the
Spirit to the Father.

One in Being with the Father

Of all the phrases used in the Creed, this seem-
ingly innocuous one was the most controversial.
Some of its significance in the Greek original was
lost in the English translation, "one in being," but
is being restored in the new liturgical translation
as "consubstantial with the Father." This takes into
account the fact that the Greek term *homoousios*
in the original – and the corresponding Latin
term *consubstantia* – use a particular term which
we might more accurately translate as "of one
substance." And so the Creed states that the Son
is "one substance" or "consubstantial" with the
Father. What was controversial, and remains so
for some, is the use of the philosophical term
"substance" in a Christian Creed. Even the fathers
of the council expressed reservations about the

use of the term, but in the end conceded the necessity of its use. Their opponents, the followers of Arius, had used the term "substance" as well, and the only way to address their argument was to use the same term they had used. We shall explore the meaning of this term later on, but note that in the context of the Creed what is being affirmed in this phrase is a repetition of what is already being said, that the Son is God, Light and true God. The Son is God in every way that the Father is God – not a second-rate or subordinate divinity or a mere creature.

The cumulative effect of this paragraph of the Creed is a strong affirmation of the full divinity of the Son. Two further points require comment.

First, belief in the Trinity is usually expressed as belief in one God and three Persons. Yet the Creed does not mention the word "person." I have used it above as a way of distinguishing between the Father and the Son. The Father is a different Person from the Son, even as they share the same divine substance. While the term "person" does not appear in the Creed it became part of the theological language to describe what it is that each of the Father, Son and Spirit are, in their divine unity. Nonetheless it is important not to over-read the meaning of the term. We should not think that we immediately know what it means, and while we can draw analogies from our understanding of personhood, these can also mislead us. When the great theologian Augustine comments on the meaning of the term "person" in relation to Father, Son and Spirit, he simply says, "Person is what there are three of in the Trinity" (*De Trinitate*, 5.10). The term "person" designates the distinction, but tells us very little else.

The second point to comment on is the relationship between what the Creed is talking about here and the Jesus we meet in the Gospels. This particular paragraph is about the Son eternally begotten of the Father (John 1:1, 14). There is a further question to ask about the relationship between the Word/Son eternally with the Father (John 1:1) and the Jesus who walked and talked in Galilee (John 1:14). This issue is taken up in the second half of the creedal affirmation concerning the Son, "for us and for our salvation he came down from heaven . . ." This teaching of the Creed found more precise expression in the teaching of a later council, that of Chalcedon (451 AD). Traditionally this is a christological issue, which is not the focus of this present work. Here I simply note that, while historically we move from our experience of Jesus, his life, death and resurrection, to consider questions of his divinity, the starting point of the teaching of the Creed is the pre-existent divinity of Jesus, then there is a move onto the question of his mission "for us and our salvation." This is perfectly legitimate because that was the question the church needed to address at the time.

We can now turn our attention to the teaching on the Holy Spirit. This is not as well developed as the teaching on the Son, and there was some clarification of that teaching in the period between the Council of Nicaea and that of Constantinople. The text which we have handed down to us is as follows:

> We believe in the Holy Spirit, the Lord, the giver of life,
> who proceeds from the Father [and the Son].
> With the Father and the Son he is worshipped and glorified.

As we can see, this teaching is not as fulsome as that on the Son. The Spirit too is referred to as the Lord, a title of divinity. The Spirit is worshipped and glorified equally with the Father and the Son. These are affirmations of the divinity of the Spirit, as it would be idolatrous to glorify and worship the Spirit as we glorify and worship the Father and the Son if the Spirit were not equal in divinity to Father and Son. As we noted above, the Creed also introduces the term "procession" to speak of the relationship between Father and Spirit. Most of us would automatically add "and the Son" to specify the relationship of the Spirit to the Father, and so in the West we generally say the Spirit "proceeds

from the Father *and the Son*." This additional
phrase, known by its Latin translation *filioque*,
represents a major dividing point between Eastern
and Western churches. It was not part of the
original Creed, but was added later on in the West,
partly due to the authority of Augustine. We shall
explore why it arises later on, but in the West, as
in the East, there is no intention to diminish the
claims of the divinity of the Spirit.

Again we note that the term "person" is not
used in relation to the Spirit, but it remains the
accepted designation for the distinctions within
the Godhead. Also the Creed does not use the
term "substance" as it did in relation to the Son.
Nonetheless the term *homoousios/consubstantia*
was used legitimately by theologians also in
relation to the divinity of the Spirit, on the same
grounds as its application to the Son. If the Spirit
is truly divine as the Son is truly divine, in every
way equal to the Father, then just as the Father
and the Son are consubstantial, so too the Spirit is
consubstantial with the Father and the Son.

To summarize, what can we say that the
Creed teaches us about the Trinity? The Creed
teaches "one God" and a threefold distinction (of
Persons) between Father, Son and Spirit. While
the Creed does not use the term "person" it has
been used and honored by the tradition to refer
to what Father, Son and Spirit are as distinct

from one another. And so the Creed affirms one God and three Persons. Each of these Persons is equally God, and they are of "one substance," or of one divine nature. Finally the Creed teaches certain relationships between the distinct Persons. The Son is begotten by the Father, and the Spirit proceeds from the Father [and the Son]. As a doctrinal shorthand we may say, "One God, three Persons, two processions."

One Substance – What Does it Mean?

As we noted above, the Creed uses the term "substance" to speak of what is common to Father and Son. The Father and the Son are "one substance." We also noted above that, at the time, even the bishops at the council found it a difficult term to use, largely because it was not scriptural. We know historically that when they left the Council of Nicaea and went back to their dioceses, many bishops found they were unable to explain to their people the meaning of the term. The term continues to be controversial. One theologian of the early twentieth century famously described its use by the council as the corruption of the pure spirit of the Gospel by Greek philosophy. Others have spoken of the need to "dehellenize" the teaching to remove such influences. On the other hand it is possible to argue that far from adopting a term with a fixed meaning from Greek philosophy, the use of the term by the council requires a new meaning to emerge for the term, one which goes beyond the limitations of the Greek philosophy of the day. <u>Far from being the hellenization of Christianity, it is more a matter of the christianization of Hellenism.</u>

Without ignoring the importance of such questions I propose a more direct study of the term itself and why it might be considered a problem. Let us consider common English usage of the term "substance." I often ask my students what is the first thing that comes to their mind when they hear the word. The common answer is along the lines of "chemical substance," or something that they could get their hands stuck in. I usually propose the term "stuff" as a synonym for this meaning of the word "substance." And so, if we think along these lines, to say the Father and the Son are of one substance we would be saying something like "they are made from the same 'God stuff.' " We can get a sense of this in the writing of the second-century church father Tertullian (ca. 160–220 AD), who spoke of the Son as "emitted" from the substance of the Father (*Against Praxeas*, Chap. 7). We might call this a materialistic reading of the word "substance" and we may well wonder if this is really what the council meant in using the term.

However, there is another meaning of the term "substance," one not so common but certainly part of standard English usage. A lawyer may get up in court and say something like, "The substance of my argument is . . ." Or we might say of a debater that she made a "substantial" point in the debate. Here we do not have in mind the sort of materialistic connotations of substance as stuff. Rather we are saying something different, something about intelligence and reason. The lawyer is trying to express the key point or insight upon which his argument hangs. Similarly a debater who makes a substantial point is shedding new light on the debate and brings a new insight to bear upon the argument. This is a very different meaning from the materialist sense of the term, and it helps shed more light on what the council meant in using the term.

Indeed if we consider the term "substance" we can break it up into "sub" and "stance." "Sub" of course means "under" and "stance" is where we stand. Some philosophers have promoted the notion that substance means "that which stands under"; however it makes more sense to me to keep the original order of the two pieces and say " 'substance' is that which we correctly understand." We might call this a more "spiritual" sense of the term. Indeed this is the sense of the word given it by Athanasius (293–373 AD), who

attended the Council of Nicaea and spent much
of his life as a bishop defending its teaching.
When asked to explain the meaning of the term
he answered along the following lines: "To say
the Father and the Son are one substance means
that whatever is true of the Father is true of the
Son, except the Father is not the Son, nor the
Son the Father" (cf. *Against the Arians*, Discourse
III.4). What Athanasius meant by this is "what
Scripture teaches as true of the Father, it also
teaches as true of the Son." And so if Scripture
teaches that the Father is eternal, it also teaches
that the Son is eternal; if the Father is creator, the
Son is also creator; if the Father is almighty, the
Son is also almighty. And so on. However, we can
generalize his meaning to state that "whatever is
true of the Father is also true of the Son," while
acknowledging that most of what we know as true
we derive from the Scriptures.

The problem we have with this "statement
about statements" is that it gives us no image to
hold on to. While the more materialist sense of
the term "substance" gives us a strong image, this
more "spiritual" sense of the term does not. Our
mind wants to hold onto the image of some sort
of material divine "stuff," but when we do we will
be misled. The only guidance we have is to hold
onto what is true, not what we may imagine. In
that sense the teaching of Nicaea requires us to ask

about what our criteria for reality are. Do we find it in suitable images or in correct understanding? If we are to understand what Nicaea means by saying that the Father and the Son are "one substance" then we must opt for the "correct understanding" rather than a "suitable image."

We may conclude then by saying that when the Creed teaches that the Father and the Son (and the Spirit) are of "one substance" what is meant is that whatever is true of the Father is true of the Son (and the Spirit). Further, we predominantly learn what is true of the Father, Son and Spirit from the Scriptures. And so just as the Father is almighty, so too are the Son and the Spirit; just as the Father is to be glorified, so too are the Son and the Spirit; and just as the Father is truly the one God, so too are the Son and the Spirit. Still the question remains, how are the Father, Son and Spirit distinct?

The Processions and the Logic of Relations

The question of how we can make distinctions within the one divine existence or substance is a difficult and profound one, but it is one in which we find some assistance from the Creed. We have already noted that the Creed teaches us not only one God and three Persons, but also two processions. These processions point to the fact that the Son and the Spirit both have an origin in the Father, and so are related to him as end point to source. The Son is "begotten" from the Father and the Spirit "proceeds" from the Father. This might suggest that the way to make distinctions within the Godhead is through an appeal to relations.

In fact this was the conclusion that some early church fathers came to in their debates on the Trinity. They ruled out various forms of distinction between Father, Son and Spirit. For example, we cannot say they are in different places, because God is not locally contained, or in different times, because God is eternal; they do not differ in quantity because each is equally and fully divine, nor in quality because of the equality of their substance. After exhaustive examination the fathers concluded that what differentiates Father, Son and Spirit from one another are the relations which define them. And so to modify the formula of Athanasius, whatever is true of the Father is true of the Son, *except that the Father begets the Son, and the Son is begotten by the Father*. Everything else about them is identical. And similarly with regard to the Spirit. Again we have no image to hold on to here, just a statement about statements. In the later tradition this will be expressed by saying that the Persons are "subsistent [i.e., distinctly existing] relations."

This claim is largely a restatement of the teaching of the Creed on the processions of the Son and the Spirit. <u>The two processions equate to four relations:</u> (1) the Father begets the Son; (2) the Son is begotten by the Father; (3) the Spirit proceeds from the Father [and the Son]; and (4) the Father [and the Son] breathes forth (or "spirates") the Spirit. Through these relations the Persons of the Trinity are mutually defined. The Father *is* the one who begets the Son; the Son *is* the one who is begotten by the Father. That is the complete identity of both Father and Son; that is *who* they are. Their personal identity *is* their mutual relationship.

The question which arose for the early church fathers and which can arise for us too is, if the Persons are defined by their relations to one another, how is the Son different from the Spirit? Both Son and Spirit stand in relation to the Father as end point to source. But if this is all we can say would not the Son and the Spirit be identical? How can we distinguish the Son and the Spirit? One suggestion made by the Greek fathers is to attempt to distinguish between the two relations by the type of relation itself. And so the Son is generated or begotten by the Father while the Spirit is breathed forth or spirated by the Father. This may seem like a satisfactory solution but it seeks to make a qualitative distinction between

the two processions – the two processions have
different qualities or properties to them – and
such a qualitative distinction could not be made
within the Godhead. And so the Greek fathers left
it as a mystery.

In the West Augustine pushed the matter
further. He noted that there is a difference
between the relationship of the Father to the Son
and that of the Father to the Spirit. We can say
that the Father is Father of the Son and the Son is
Son of the Father; but while we say that the Spirit
is the Spirit of the Father, we never say that the
Father is the Father of the Spirit. The first relation,
between Father and Son, is mutually defining. But
if the Father's personhood is already defined by
his relation to the Son, it cannot be defined again
by his relation to the Spirit. The only way that
Augustine could find to ensure that the identity of
the Spirit does not collapse into the identity of the
Son is to implicate the Son in the procession of the
Spirit. And so he proposed that the Spirit proceeds
from the Father *and the Son*. As we noted above,
this phrase, in Latin *filioque*, was later added to
the Creed in the West but its addition has never
been accepted by Eastern Orthodoxy.

Of course Augustine also had a scriptural
argument for the *filioque*, drawing on John 15:26,
"[The Spirit] whom I will send to you from the
Father" and John 14:26, "[The Spirit] whom the

Father will send in my name." However, for our
purposes we may derive it from Athanasius' rule.
It is true that the Spirit proceeds from the Father,
and whatever is true of the Father is true of the
Son, except the Father begets the Son and the Son
is begotten by the Father. And so it is true that
the Spirit also proceeds from the Son as well as
from the Father. This type of argument works so
long as the relationship between the Father and
the Son is mutually defining of their identity. It is
a conclusion from the logic of relations but once
again we have no image to grasp to give us an
insight into how we might understand what we
are arguing.

So through reflecting on the two processions
as taught by the Creed we can develop an
understanding of the Persons as distinguished
by their mutual relations. These four relations,
of Father to Son, Son to Father, Father and Son
to Spirit and Spirit to Father and Son, are simply
a restatement of the teaching of the processions.
Through the inner logic of relations we have
drawn a conclusion which has been accepted
in the West, but not in the East, that the Spirit
proceeds from the Father and the Son. In fact
this phrase was adopted into the Latin (Western)
version of the Creed in about the eighth century
and has remained there ever since.

Two processions giving rise to four relations

Father → Son
The Father generates the Son;
the Son is generated or proceeds from the Father.

Father + Son → Holy Spirit
The Father and Son spirate the Spirit;
the Spirit is spirated or proceeds from the Father
and the Son.

Subordination and/or Hierarchy?

One question which arises from the logic of
relations and processions is that of subordination
or hierarchy between the Persons. The Son and
the Spirit find their origin in the Father; the Son is
begotten from the Father and the Spirit is spirated
by the Father [and the Son]. Does this not make
the Father more "important" or more "divine"
than the Son and the Spirit? This is certainly
the position the church sought to reject in its
assertion of the full divinity of the Son and the
Spirit. Nonetheless it may be reinforced by the way
some theologians, particularly from the Eastern
Orthodox tradition, speak of the "monarchy
of the Father." On the other hand, the teaching
that the Son and the Spirit are of one substance
with the Father means that whatever is true of the
Father is true of the Son and the Spirit. So that

any attribute, such as power, wisdom, greatness, eternity or divinity which belongs to the Father belongs equally to the Son and the Spirit.

However, we can pursue this further by a consideration of the logic of relations. When we think of a human father and son, it does not follow that the father is more important or indeed more human than the son. In fact both are fully equal in their humanity. The relationship of father and son does not imply any hierarchy between them, or that the son is subordinate to the father. In some ways a human son may surpass his father and so be "greater" than his father in some aspect. And so saying that the Father is the source of the Son and the Spirit does not necessarily make the Father more important or more divine than the Son and the Spirit. All three remain equal in their divinity, a fact which is not negated by their mutual ordering.

Our Relations to the Persons

We have been putting forward the position that the Persons of the Trinity are defined by their mutual relations. These Persons are also in relationship with us as creator to creature. As creatures we stand in a relationship of complete dependence upon Father, Son and Spirit as the one God, creator of "all that is seen and unseen." This is a relationship which can be broken only if we were to slip into complete non-existence. God knows and loves us into existence through this relationship of creator to creature. However, this relationship is to Father, Son and Spirit equally and indistinguishably. If we could relate to Father, Son and Spirit in a distinct manner simply because of our relationship to God as our creator, then we would not need revelation to teach us of the Trinity. However, we know of God as Father, Son and Spirit only because of what is revealed in the New Testament.

In the New Testament we find hints of a different type of relationship, one which goes beyond the relationship between creature and creator. The Holy Spirit is poured into our hearts (Rom 5:5). We are made coheirs with Christ, adopted sons and daughters (Gal 4:5). We become partakers of the divine nature (2 Pet 1:4). When we die we shall see God face-to-face and know him as fully as we are known (1 Cor 13:12). All these speak of an intimacy with the divine which goes beyond the relationship of creator to creature. How can we understand this? Can we in some sense share in the relations which define the Persons through God's divine graciousness to us?

If we step back a moment from this deep question we can ask ourselves how we know about the processions of the Son and the Spirit. Indeed they are not given to us immediately in the New Testament. What we first encounter are the divine missions of the Son and the Spirit. The Son and the Spirit are sent to us "for us and our salvation." The Son is sent by the Father on the mission to proclaim the kingdom of God, and the Spirit empowers us to live out our participation in that mission as God's love poured into our hearts. The processions are revealed to us through the missions of the Son and the Spirit.

One could then argue that inasmuch as we participate in the divine missions, inasmuch as we share in the mission of Jesus to work for the building up of the kingdom and are empowered to do so by the Spirit living in our hearts, we are sharing too in the relations which define the Son and the Spirit in their relations to one another and to the Father. We become not just imitators of Christ, but share in an imitation of the divine relations, and so share in the divine trinitarian nature. This of course goes well beyond what is stated in the Creed, but it is an indication of the extraordinary privilege we have as believers in the Divine Trinity. Through the life of grace we enter into the very life of the Trinity itself through our participation in the mission of the Son and the Spirit. This is why belief in the Trinity is the defining characteristic of Christian faith. It is not just a revelation of what God is like, but also an invitation to share in the very life of God's own being.

Conclusion

In this chapter I have presented the teaching of
the Nicene Creed with some minimal theological
exposition. I have tried to keep as close to the
text and its traditional reading as possible to set
out what it is Christians believe about God as
Father, Son and Spirit. As such the content of this
chapter is largely doctrinal, specifying the "what"
of belief. However, a continual question that can
arise is: how can this be so? How can the one
God be three Persons? How can we understand
this? Here we can identify a movement to a more
explicitly theological phase where faith seeks some
form of understanding. And so we ask: how can
we understand the Trinity? Of course complete
understanding, or at least the most complete we
will ever have, lies in our seeing God face-to-face,
when we shall know as fully as we are known –
what we refer to as "the beatific vision." However,
in the next chapter we shall explore some of the
ways theologians have sought to address this
question, not directly, but by seeking analogies
for the Trinity in the created order.

CHAPTER 3

The Way of Analogy

In this chapter we turn our attention to the question: how can we understand the Trinity? From the earliest times, Christian theologians have sought to find analogies for the Trinity in created realities. To seek an analogy is one way of trying to understand something as yet unknown. We can say that X, an unknown, is like Y, something we can understand. And so we might say that an old vinyl-record player is similar to a new CD player; but in doing so we would not only point out the similarities but also the differences. In that way we can move from what is better known to what is less well known (where, in this case, what is less well known might be an indication of one's age!). Analogy is a tool of understanding which we can use to try to get a better handle on how it can be that there are three Persons in one God. This is not an attempt to prove that God is triune; rather it is an exercise in "faith seeking understanding." We believe that there are three Persons in God and we want to understand something of how this might be. However, because we are dealing with the very mystery of God, we know that any analogy we develop will necessarily fall short. And some fall shorter than others!

In undertaking this task it is important to realize that, whatever we may arrive at as an analogy, it cannot claim to be something we *must* believe. It has more the character of a theological hypothesis or theory. It will not provide us with greater certainty, but with greater understanding of what we hold with the certainty of faith. In fact this is the goal of theology proposed in the teaching of Vatican I, that is, the fruitful understanding of the mysteries of faith from analogies of what is naturally known and through interconnection of the mysteries themselves and with our final end. In this present work we are concentrating on the first of these goals, that is, seeking analogies from what is naturally known.

Perhaps the best known analogy, at least to those of Irish Catholic background, is that of St Patrick (fifth-century AD). In seeking to convert the people of Ireland, Patrick proposed an analogy based on the shamrock, a small three-leafed plant, where the three leaves emerge from a common section of the plant. In this way he sought to help common people understand the three-in-oneness of the Trinity. Of course it is not a great analogy because it implies a material sense of the sharing of the divine nature. One leaf might be bigger than another or could be torn from the main body of the plant. However, there is another major weakness to the analogy. When we summarized the teaching of the Creed, we spoke of one God, three Persons, and two processions. While the analogy of the shamrock speaks of the three-in-oneness of the Trinity it provides us with no understanding of the two processions. None of the leaves "proceeds" from any of the others, so that element of our belief remains very obscure. We might also note that it provides no understanding of why there are three Persons in God and not four or two. If one had a four-leaf shamrock, by some genetic accident, the analogy would clearly not work.

And so we might set out what we would hope an analogy might provide us with. We would want to be able to shed some light on the threefold distinction of Father, Son and Spirit in the Godhead. We might also want it to provide some insight into why there are three Persons and not two or four or whatever number one might think. We might also want some insight into the two processions – it is interesting to note in this regard that the first question Aquinas asks in relation to the Trinity is exactly this: are there processions in God? And as with the number of Persons we might also want to get some insight into why there are two processions and not one or three. These might be considered to be the basic requirements of a good analogy.

Some Early Examples of Analogies

The early church fathers developed a number of simple analogies which sought to give some understanding of the Trinity. One developed by Irenaeus (second-century AD) spoke of the Son and the Spirit as the two hands of the Father. He drew upon the notion that human beings are made in the image and likeness of God, so that just as we have two hands, so too does God. Through these two "hands" God accomplishes what needs to be done in creation and for our redemption. While this is a nice image it clearly falls short in many ways. Our hands are a part of us, while the Son and the Spirit are not parts of God: they are fully God. The image of hands seems to imply that the Son and the Spirit are subordinate to the Father, that the Father is fully God while the Son and the Spirit are not the full deal. It is this type of subordination that the Creed of Nicaea sought to rule out when it taught that the Son is "God from God, Light from Light, true God from true God, of one substance with the Father." Also it is not clear how the Son and the Spirit "proceed" from the Father; they are more like attachments and the image does not capture the dynamism of procession. Of course we cannot criticize Irenaeus for these shortcomings. He wrote before the clarity of Nicaea was achieved and was doing the best he could at the time.

A further set of images or analogies was provided by Tertullian. He was a complex character who provided the church with some of its most enduring terminology in dealing with the Trinity. He spoke of there being one "substance" though he tended to understand it in a materialistic sense. He also spoke of the three as persons. While he held to a true belief in the Trinity his theological explanations often left something to be desired. In his later life he left the church and joined a more rigorous and enthusiastic group of Christians known as Montanists. However, in his teaching on the Trinity he introduced the following images:

> For God sent forth the Word, as the Paraclete also declares, just as the root puts forth the tree, and the fountain the river, and the sun the ray. For these are *emanations* of the substances from which they proceed. I should not hesitate, indeed, to call the tree the son or offspring of the root, and the river of the fountain, and the ray of the sun; because every original source is a parent, and everything which issues from the origin is an offspring . . . But still the tree is not severed from the root, nor the river from the fountain, nor the ray from the sun; nor, indeed,

is the Word separated from God. Following,
therefore, the form of these analogies, I confess
that I call God and His Word – the Father and
His Son – *two*. For the root and the tree are
distinctly two things, but correlatively joined;
the fountain and the river are also two forms,
but indivisible; so likewise the sun and the ray
are two forms, but coherent ones. Everything
which proceeds from something else must
needs be second to that from which it proceeds,
without being on that account separated:
Where, however, there is a second, there must
be two; and where there is a third, there must
be three. Now the Spirit indeed is third from
God and the Son; just as the fruit of the tree
is third from the root, or as the stream out of
the river is third from the fountain, or as the
apex of the ray is third from the sun. Nothing,
however, is alien from that original source
whence it derives its own properties.
(*Against Praxeas*, Chap. 8)

These sets of images, which I have quoted at
some length, become something of the stock-in-
trade of many of the early church fathers when
they seek to present analogies for the Trinity.
One of the advantages they have over the image
of the two hands is that they seek to capture
something of the dynamism of the processions
through images of flow and growth. But like the
analogy provided by St Patrick they suffer from

being materialistic in their basic starting points. They speak either of separate things or of distinct elements which are parts of a larger thing, and neither case is what we find in the Trinity. And so while they are interesting analogies they also have major weaknesses.

A different type of analogy was provided by a later theologian, Origen (185–254 AD). He was more sophisticated philosophically and could see the limitations of the type of material images that had been used by others to shed light on the mystery of the Trinity. Reflecting on the teaching of Genesis that human beings are made in the image and likeness of God, he sought an analogy not in the physical make-up of our bodies, as had Irenaeus, but in the spiritual operations of the mind. And so in seeking to understand how the Father can generate a Son he spoke of "the image of the Father formed in the Son, who is born of Him, like an act of His will proceeding from the mind" (*De Principiis*, I, 2, 6). By focusing on the operations of the mind and will, Origen shifted attention from the outer world of materiality into the more spiritual realm of human operations of knowing and willing. This marks an important development.

This development is further refined by one of the Cappadocian fathers, Gregory of Nyssa (ca. 335–394 AD). When trying to understand how the Father could generate a Son he draws upon an analogy from the operations of the mind:

> In a human context we say that a word comes from the mind, being neither completely identical with the mind nor utterly different from it: for it is distinct, as being from it; yet it cannot be conceived as different, since it reveals the mind itself; it is in nature identical with the mind but distinct, as being a separate subject. Similarly the Word of God. (*Oratio Catechetica*, 1.2)

How then does the Spirit fit into this analogy? Gregory speaks of the Spirit as analogous to a human breath accompanying the production of the spoken word. We are a long way here from Tertullian's images of trees, fountains and sunlight. Gregory's analogies are more "personal" in that they relate to operations of persons, rather than impersonal objects. They reflect the biblical teaching that human beings are made in the image and likeness of God and so seek to find analogies for the Trinity in human beings. However, there is also a weakness here because, while Gregory has found an interesting spiritual analogy for the procession of the Son or Word of God, when it comes to the procession of the Spirit he resorts to a more materialistic image of breath accompanying a spoken word.

These developments, which we find in the

work of Origen and Gregory, lay the groundwork for a more fully developed analogy which emerges in the writings of Augustine, one of the greatest theologians of the Western tradition. It is to this that we now turn.

The Psychological Analogy

Perhaps the highest point of theological attempts to find a suitable analogy occurs in the major work on the Trinity by Augustine, entitled simply *On the Trinity* (*De Trinitate*). It is a complex and profound work which took over twenty years for Augustine to complete. In many ways the structure of this present work parallels the structure of Augustine's book, for he begins with Scripture, then considers the more technical terms of "substance" and "relations," before moving to what he refers to as a more "inward manner" of exploration. His reasons for this interior exploration follow what we have already spoken of above, that human beings are made in the image and likeness of God, and so we can turn to the spiritual aspects of human beings in our attempts to find a suitable analogy for the Trinity. Centuries later Thomas Aquinas will follow Augustine in further developing and refining this analogy.

Of course if we are seeking an analogy between two things we presume one of them is understood, or at least better understood, than the other. If this were not the case then the analogy would shed no light. So the first problem we encounter in this attempted analogy is the question: just how well do we know our own interior operations? Most of us may say we know about this or that, we understand various things, but if we are to develop this analogy we must know about knowing and understand understanding. We must learn to attend to the things that happen within us as we understand, or make judgments or decisions. It is not common for people to attend to such things and it is not necessarily an easy thing to do, as Augustine was well aware. We all have a mind and we all use our mind every day, but we rarely attend to its functioning. We generally leave such questions to philosophers and psychologists. But if we are to understand what is being asked of us here we must learn to attend to certain inner operations.

What operations does Augustine want us to attend to? The sorts of things he has in mind are the following: coming to give a definition of something; coming to express approval or disapproval, or what we would call forming a judgment of value; and coming to a decision for either sinning or doing good. Each of these involves a certain movement in the mind which is not a material movement – we do not necessarily get up and move about – but something within

us "shifts" as the mind comes to a certain "point."
We even speak of the mind conceiving a concept,
using the same word which we use to speak of
the formation of new life, conception. A new
concept emerges from the fact that we understand
something for the first time. This concept is the end
point of an interior movement which Augustine
refers to as an "inner word." It is not the word
we speak, but an inner word, the end point of a
movement from understanding to inner concept.

My preferred example is more by way of the
formation of a judgment, particularly a judgment
of value, which Augustine refers to as "knowledge
with love":

> The kind of word then that we are now wishing
> to distinguish and propose is "knowledge with
> love." So when the mind knows and loves itself,
> its word is joined to it with love. And since it
> loves knowledge and knows love, the word is in
> the love and the love is in the word and both in
> the lover and the utterer. (*De Trinitate*, 9.15)

When we make a judgment of value we set about
to weigh the evidence, looking at the pros and
cons, asking further questions and exploring
further possibilities. But there comes a time when
it all comes together for us, when all the evidence
we need has come in, when all our relevant
questions and concerns have been addressed; and
the mind comes to a point of finality, of closure

and moves to an inner judgment. That inner word of judgment then finds expression in an outer word, "Yes!" This is his analogy for understanding the generation or procession of the Son or Word of God as knowledge with love.

Augustine is often criticized by people who say that this analogy is not scriptural. Of course the same criticism was raised by those who thought the Council of Nicaea should not use the term "substance" because it was not scriptural. However, I think that Augustine is in fact reflecting on two very profound scriptural texts. The first is John 1:1: "In the beginning was the Word, and the Word was with God, and the Word was God." This reference to the Divine Son as the Word of God might ask us to reflect on how God might have such an inner word, a word which is not separate from God and is itself divine. It is not difficult to think that this type of question is behind what Augustine (and Gregory of Nyssa before him) was thinking about when he formulated this analogy. The other text is from Paul: 2 Corinthians 1:20: "For in him [Jesus] every one of God's promises is a 'Yes.' " Jesus is the "Yes" of God, the "Yes" through whom all creation has come into being, the "Yes" of salvation spoken on the cross, the "Yes" of our final judgment when we die. This is the inner word of God, an inner judgment of value, which affirms the divine goodness, and everything that divine goodness does. This inner word finds outer expression in the Word incarnate in Jesus of Nazareth (John 1:14).

However, as the quote from Augustine above indicates, this is not the end of the story (or the analogy). For while Gregory of Nyssa spoke of the Spirit as the breath which accompanied the speaking of the Word, and we noted that this was a more materialist analogy which might need some refining, we can see from the quote from Augustine above that he speaks of "knowledge with love." When we come to that inner judgment of value, when we say an inner "Yes" to something that we judge to be good, then it releases a proper love for that object which we have judged to be good. We can "appreciate" the object, resting in its goodness, giving forth an inner "sigh" of contentment. This is Augustine's analogy for the procession of the Spirit: not the outer breath with the spoken word but the inner sigh of divine contentment that is released by the Word as a judgment of value.

There is a psychological rule that Augustine regularly quotes when speaking of the procession of the Spirit in relation to the generation of the Word. He repeatedly states that "nothing is loved unless it is first known." It is worth thinking about this for a while because it is saying something important about the nature of the procession of

the Spirit. Often Augustine's analogy is expressed
as involving the mind and the will, and this is part
of the truth, but it hides the intimate connection
between knowing and willing that he is seeking
to draw. When Augustine says nothing is loved
unless it is first known, it is not as if he is unaware
that we love many things without really knowing
them. Often we say "Love is blind," implying
that, if we really knew, we would not love. But
he is talking about something deeper which we
might express by saying "Nothing is responsibly
loved unless it is known." He is not talking
about silly, irresponsible love or infatuations, but
about mature, responsible love which commits
itself because it really understands what it is
committing to. And so the love that is analogous
to the procession of the Spirit is not any old love,
but a responsible, mature, well-grounded love,
love grounded in the truth. It is worth noting that
this observation of Augustine is the psychological
equivalent of the *filioque* – that the Spirit proceeds
from the Father *and the Son*.

Again it is not as if we cannot find scriptural
support for such a position. Paul speaks of God's
love that "has been poured into our hearts through
the Holy Spirit that has been given to us" (Rom
5:5). Just as the Spirit is God's love given to us, so
too the Spirit is the inner, responsible divine Love
released by the inner Word of judgment spoken by

the Father. Paul also speaks of the Spirit helping us in our weakness, interceding with "sighs too deep for words" (Rom 8:26). In such sighing do we not participate in the very divine sighing that the Spirit is, the sighing of contentment in the divine goodness? Is this not part of our participation in the divine nature (2 Pet 1:4)?

There is of course much more work that needs to be done. We would need to argue that the judgment expressed in the Word is nothing less than God. This is not the case in our human knowing, which is limited. But Augustine argues that, because God's knowledge is perfect and the expression of that knowledge in the Divine Word is perfect, God's Word is not less than God: "the Word was with God, and the Word was God" (John 1:1). A similar, if perhaps less persuasive, argument can be made in relation to the Spirit. It is clear that the analogy is stretching us to our limits in these matters. Augustine is indeed asking us to go to the very limits of our human experiences of knowing and loving. Also for us these events may be separated in time, or at least follow a temporal sequence; again this is not the case with regard to God, in whom the three acts of Understanding, expressing a Word and sighing the Spirit are simultaneous. No one Person is temporally "before" the other, but we still think of the Father as the source of the Son and the Spirit.

It is not uncommon to criticize Augustine's analogy on the basis that it is based on a single human subject. This is a concern that he too notes. Some have argued (incorrectly I think) that this focus on the operations of a single subject is the source of modern individualism. On the other hand we can ask what Augustine achieves in this analogy. He presents an understanding of a threefold distinction between the understanding Subject (the Father), the Word spoken by that Subject, and the Spirit sighed through the Word by the same Subject. The threefold distinction is not arbitrary but reflects the operations of the subject. It also helps us understand the three Persons and two processions in terms of those operations. These are dynamic operations of the conceiving of the Word and the breathing forth of the Spirit, operations that are understood analogously in terms of processes of knowing and willing. All in all it is a pretty good effort and certainly much better than the alternatives around both in Augustine's time and today.

One important feature of this analogy, however, deserves our attention. The analogy locates an image of God in every human being, male or female, child or adult, saint or sinner. As Augustine himself says:

> Therefore, if it is with reference to its capacity
> to use reason and understanding in order to

understand and gaze upon God that it was
made to the image of God, it follows that from
the moment this great and wonderful nature
begins to be, this image is always there, whether
it is so worn away as to be almost nothing, or
faint and distorted, or clear and beautiful. (*De
Trinitate*, 14.6)

This is a powerful statement of the dignity of every
human being, made in the image and likeness of
God, carrying within every one of us an image of
the Divine Trinity. No other analogy can say this
with such force and clarity.

Wisdom and Love

In the end what the psychological analogy is
asking us to contemplate is the relationship
between wisdom or intelligence and love. Given
the basics of the analogy we may speak of the
Divine Word as the Loving Wisdom of God and
the Divine Spirit as the Wise Loving of God. God
the Father, as the primordial state of love ("God is
love" – 1 John 4:8), speaks forth the divine Loving
Wisdom of the Word which directs and releases
the Wise Loving of the Spirit. This is not quite
what Augustine is saying but it is consonant with
it. It finds its inspiration in the writings of a more
recent theologian, Bernard Lonergan (1904–
1984). But in both Augustine's and Lonergan's
analogies we have this interconnection between

Wisdom and Love, between Loving Wisdom and Wise Loving.

These two aspects reflect lessons we need to learn in the contemporary age. Too often intelligence and reason are reduced to mere calculation, profit and loss, advantage and disadvantage, pleasure and pain. We even begin to think of human beings as being like computers and we seek to develop analogies between the human mind and microchips, between human cognition and binary calculations. We have stripped the mind of its flesh and blood, of its deeper understanding and empathy for its object. We need to restore a deeper meaning to our understanding of the human mind, not in terms of calculation but in terms of wisdom, a loving wisdom that appreciates the fully human nature of our situation, that can feel our plight from the inside and not reduce us to entries in an accountant's ledger. As Christians, we believe Jesus is the embodiment of the Loving Wisdom of God, who knows fully what it is to be human "from the inside."

On the other side of the equation we know that love has become one of the more debased words in our language. People fall in and out of love on a regular basis. They love their cars, their pets, their computers and every possible item of fashion. Love, like fashion, is fickle or at least so it seems. Yet we long for a more profound sense of love, firmly based, grounded in something more than mere whim, a faithful and committed love which does not change with the seasons or time of day. Again we need to restore a deeper meaning to our understanding of love, not in terms of blind impulse towards the other, but as a responsible and committed act, an act of wise loving which truly knows both itself and the beloved, and which offers its love wisely out of that true knowledge. The Spirit is God's Wise Loving poured into our hearts, empowering us to love wisely and not foolishly, firmly and not on a whim.

Pope Benedict XVI expresses some of these concerns in his encyclical *Caritas in Veritate* ("Love in Truth"). As the title suggests, Benedict is concerned with the intimate connection between truth and love, a connection we find in the psychological analogy. As he states it:

> The demands of love do not contradict those of reason. Human knowledge is insufficient and the conclusions of science cannot indicate by themselves the path towards integral human development. There is always a need to push further ahead: this is what is required by charity in truth. Going beyond, however, never means prescinding from the conclusions of reason, nor contradicting its results. Intelligence and love are not in separate compartments: *love is*

rich in intelligence and intelligence is full of
love. (*Caritas in Veritate,* no. 30; emphasis in
the original)

This is the basic insight from the psychological
analogy: *divine love is rich in intelligence and
divine intelligence is full of love.* This is a truth
manifest in God and dimly reflected in ourselves
as made in the divine image.

Conclusion

This concludes our direct study of the Trinity.
We have moved from its basis in the Scriptures,
through its exposition in the Creed of Nicaea,
to its theological elaboration by Augustine. As
believing Christians the first two of these steps
give a normative expression to Christian faith.
The last element, its theological elaboration, is
simply one attempt to grasp some understanding
of the doctrine, to understand how it can be so.
There are other such attempts, of greater or lesser
success, but this one has served the Catholic
theological tradition for over one thousand five
hundred years and deserves to be taken seriously.
Nonetheless one can take it or leave it as a possible
understanding – if you find it illuminating, all the
better; if you do not, you may need to seek one
elsewhere.

There are two points I would like to make
in concluding this study. The first concerns the

difficulties facing contemporary belief in the Trinity. In a world where even believing in God can be difficult enough, Christians in general are poorly informed on what it is they believe in relation to the Trinity. The rise of Islam in the West is enough to remind us that it is far easier to proclaim and defend belief in one God than it is to proclaim and defend three Persons in one God. It is too easy for Christians to slide into a vague unitarian position, or to view the Persons as simply manifestations of the one God, rather than viewing them as distinctions within God's own being. And so our study has focused not on how we experience God, but on how God is in God's own being. For Christian belief goes beyond what we experience of God to speak of how God actually is, as Father, Son and Spirit. It can do this only because God has so revealed it to us, through the Scriptures, and through the faith of the church.

The second and perhaps more important point is to say again what a remarkable privilege God has granted us as Christians in revealing this aspect of the divine life. And this revelation is also an invitation to share in, to participate in, this life. Through the life of grace we can participate in the missions of the Son and the Spirit, imitating their own intimate relationships with one another and the Father. Our hope is that, when our life comes to its end, we may see God face-to-face and that the full depths of the mystery of the Trinity of Wisdom and Love will be revealed to us.

APPENDIX 1

The Trinity and Gender

For most of Christian history the question of the
gender specification of the Persons of the Trinity
has not been an issue. The traditional designation
of the Persons as "Father, Son and Holy Spirit"
has not given rise to problems. The names
"Father" and "Son" clearly have a male reference,
but it is interesting to note that some of the early
church fathers used feminine pronouns to speak
of the Spirit. However, with the rise of the modern
feminist movement and a new recognition of the
equal dignity of women – having the vote, equal
pay for equal work, access to education, and so on
– there has been increasing unease among some
with the traditional designation, which seems to
make God masculine. As one feminist theologian
has suggested, "If God is male, then male is god."
Thinking of God as male seems to some to embed
gender inequality and certainly make a man more
in the "image and likeness of God" than a woman
can claim to be.

Two things need to be said at the outset. The first is that, as pure spirit, God is neither male nor female (cf. *Catechism of the Catholic Church*, no. 239). Male and female genders arise from our biological constitution and God has no such biology; God is pure spirit, immaterial, and so has no gender. The same can be said individually of the Persons of the Trinity. Though the names "Father" and "Son" might appear to indicate male gender, in fact what they specify is the relationship of Father and Son. And so the Father begets the Son and the Son is begotten of the Father. The names are expressions of this mutual relationship in terms of origin and end point, rather than expressions of the gender of the Persons. And so the Eleventh Council of Toledo (675 AD) declared that the Son proceeds out of the *womb* of the Father! This makes it obvious how little the terms have any clear gender reference.

The second thing that needs to be said is that the names "Father" and "Son" are deeply embedded in the tradition; indeed they come from Jesus himself. Any attempt to replace these terms must come to grips with this origin in Jesus' own practice of referring to himself as "Son" and to God as "Father." Christian belief is based on this tradition and it needs to be respected. However, these are not the only terms used within the New Testament, especially in relation to the

Son. As we have seen regularly in this work, the New Testament also refers to the Son as the Word (John 1:1). We shall return to this observation in a moment, but before that we should attend to the difficulties that arise from one of the alternative formulas people have used to avoid the gender reference for the Persons of the Trinity.

In seeking to avoid the use of gender-specific terms for the Persons of the Trinity some have proposed a formula such as "Creator, Redeemer, and Sanctifier." And so this has been used as an alternative baptismal formula in some situations. The difficulty with this form of words is that it is not actually a trinitarian formula. The distinctions between Father, Son and Spirit do not correspond to the distinctions between God as creator, redeemer and sanctifier. First, as we noted in Chapter 2, while the Creed speaks of the Father as maker, it also gives the Son and the Spirit a role in creation. In Western theology, Father, Son and Spirit are equally Creator, and arguably equally Redeemer and Sanctifier. Second, the terms proposed, "Creator," "Redeemer" and "Sanctifier," do not specify the relationships between the Persons, especially the relationship between Father and Son. We get no sense with such terms that one Person is the source, the other the one who proceeds. In this way the proposed formula does not express the inner divine nature of the distinctions between the Persons. The designations "Creator," "Redeemer" and "Sanctifier" all speak of God's activities in relation to the created order, while the names "Father," "Son" and "Spirit" seek to designate the inner divine relations between the Persons. So, whatever we might make of the intentions of those who utilize such a formula as "Creator, Redeemer and Sanctifier," it does not express the trinitarian faith of the Christian tradition.

Is there then a valid alternative to the traditional designation of the Persons as Father, Son and Spirit which is not gender-specific? We have already noted above the well-accepted designation of the Second Person of the Trinity as the Word of God. This is clearly gender-neutral. What we then need is a term which stands to the Word as Father stands to the Son. While not commonly used in the tradition the obvious solution would be to refer to the First Person of the Trinity as the Speaker, the Speaker of the Word. The pairing "Speaker and Word" expresses the same relationship as Father and Son. In fact Aquinas occasionally refers to the First Person of the Trinity as the Speaker, so its use has some currency in the tradition. And so the formula "Speaker, Word and Spirit" could be used as an alternative, gender-neutral way of expressing the same realities as "Father, Son and Spirit."

Homily Notes
for Trinity Sunday

Trinity Sunday presents particular challenges to most homilists. Often when they did their seminary studies the course on the Trinity was considered difficult and obscure. They come to Trinity Sunday with one thought foremost in their mind, "The Trinity is a mystery," and little that they are going to say is likely to shed much light on the topic. The purpose of this appendix is to provide some homily notes that might help the potential homilist to work with the readings provided by the Lectionary to bring their congregation to a deeper appreciation of the meaning of the doctrine of the Trinity in their lives.

Apart from the readings there are other resources which the homilist can draw upon in constructing his homily. These include the Creed, the Gloria and the Eucharistic Prayer, all of which the congregation will be familiar with. These provide a field of meaning, a range of allusions, which form part of the trinitarian identity of the congregation. But a central insight is the privilege we have of knowing the Trinity, that God has chosen to reveal to us something of what we could never otherwise know: that God is Father, Son and Spirit.

Year A

Readings

- Exodus 34:4-6, 8-9: God is full of tenderness and compassion, slow to anger, rich in kindness and faithfulness.
- 2 Corinthians 13:11-13: The grace of the Lord Jesus Christ, the love of God and the fellowship of the Holy Spirit.
- John 3:16-18: God so loved the world that he gave his only Son.

Homily Notes

These readings may cause us to reflect on the unique privilege of Christian faith. The beginnings of this privilege are already present in the history of the chosen people, who experience God as full of compassion and tenderness. God walks with them, leading them out of the desert. This same compassion and tenderness is revealed in a most surprising fashion in the New Testament through an outpouring of grace, love and fellowship given to us as believers. God's love for us is so great that God shares with us the intimacy of the divine life.

God's relationship to us in various ways as Father, Son and Spirit are not just ways in which God chooses to relate to us "for us and our salvation" but ways which reflect something of the mystery of God's own being. The God who loves the world so much that he gives his only Son does not give us something less than God, but gives us the fully Divine Son. The God who offers us the fellowship of the Divine Spirit does not give us something less than God, but the Spirit that is truly and fully God. Of all the religious faiths in the world, our Christian faith is the only one to whom this mystery has been revealed.

Year B

Readings

- Deuteronomy 4:32-34, 39-40: Did ever a people hear the voice of the living God speaking from the heart of the fire?
- Romans 8:14-17: The spirit you received is the spirit of sons [and daughters!] and it makes us cry out "Abba, Father!"
- Matthew 28:16-20: Baptize them in the name of the Father, Son and Holy Spirit.

Homily Notes

These readings, particularly the gospel, may lead us to reflect on the teaching of the Creed that Father, Son and Spirit are all equally God and the

one God. The baptismal formula is an expression
of the complete equality of Father, Son and Spirit.
They are all on the same "level," so to speak, or
as the Creed says, they are "of one substance/
being." However, this belief is not just a statement
about how God is: it is a living revelation to us
"from the heart of the divine fire." It is not just
something we know, but something we are meant
to live: in prayer, making us cry out "Abba Father";
and in discipleship, spreading the Good News of
God's kingdom to all peoples. Inasmuch as we
participate in these missions of Son and Spirit we
not only know God as Father, Son and Spirit (cf.
the Creed), but we imitate the Son and the Spirit
and so participate in the divine life. Inasmuch as
we so participate in the divine life in the here and
now we hope to share in the divine life when we
die and so see God face-to-face.

Year C

Readings

- Proverbs 8:22-31: Wisdom is with God from
  the beginning of creation.
- Romans 5:1-5: God's love has been poured into
  our hearts by the Holy Spirit given to us.
- John 16:12-15: The Spirit will lead us to
  complete truth.

Homily Notes

These readings can form a natural entry point to talk about some aspects of the psychological analogy and the relationship between truth and love. Starting with reflections on divine Wisdom we are led to a consideration of the Spirit as divine Love poured into our hearts and of the Spirit as leading us to complete truth. Jesus is divine Wisdom and Truth incarnate and so the Spirit leads us to Jesus and Jesus sends us his Spirit. These experiences of the divine presence in Jesus and the Spirit can lead us to consider the distinctions within God's own being of Wisdom and Love. Following Benedict XVI we can say, "Intelligence and love are not in separate compartments: *love is rich in intelligence and intelligence is full of love.*" God's Intelligence is manifest in his Word or Wisdom, his Love in the Spirit; as the Father speaks forth the Word, his divine "Yes" to all that God is and does, the Divine Spirit is released in the deep sigh of divine contentment, a contentment we shall share when our hearts rest in God (cf. Augustine). These reflections might lead to a consideration of the ways we think of intelligence as devoid of love and of love as devoid of intelligence, and so to reconsider our ways of thinking and loving to make them more attuned to the loving Wisdom and wise Loving of God.

Glossary

Beatific vision: the direct vision of God enjoyed by the saints in heaven, where we see God "face-to-face."

Church councils: gatherings of bishops which meet to determine matters of church doctrine and discipline. There were seven "ecumenical councils" in the early church which formulated our main trinitarian and christological doctrines.

Economy (of salvation): the ways in which God operates in history to bring about our salvation, through the life, death and resurrection of Jesus and the outpouring of his Spirit.

Filioque: a Latin expression for "and the Son," a term added to the Creed of Nicaea in the West to clarify the manner of the procession of the Spirit from the Father *and the Son* (*filioque*).

Generate/generation: refers to the belief that the Father generates the Son and that the Son is begotten of the Father. It is drawn from the

Greek text of John 1:14, which refers to the Son as *monogenous* or "only begotten" of the Father.

Hellenism: a term used to refer to the impact of Greek (Hellenic) culture and philosophy on Christian practices and belief.

Incarnate/Incarnation: refers to the specific Christian belief that the Word of God (Logos or Son) took on human existence or was "in the flesh" (in Latin, *in carno*). More generally we can talk about the way people "incarnate" specific values or ways of life.

Modalism/modalist: a particular distortion of Christian belief in the Trinity which views the distinctions between Father, Son and Spirit as *modes* of God's revelation to us, not as representing real distinctions within God's own being.

Monotheism: belief in the existence of one God. Judaism, Christianity and Islam are monotheistic faiths.

Polytheism: belief in the existence of many gods.

Pre-existent: refers to the notion that the Word or Son existed "before" the Incarnation as Jesus of Nazareth, that is, that which existed personally as Jesus of Nazareth existed eternally as the Son or Word of God.

Procession: refers to the belief that both the Son and the Spirit have their origins in the Father, so that both the Son and the Spirit *proceed* from the Father.

Relation: the four divine relations are simply the two processions, plus the inverse of each procession; and so the Son proceeds from or is generated by the Father, while the Father generates the Son; the Spirit proceeds from or *is spirated* by the Father and the Son, while the Father and the Son *spirate* the Spirit.

Spirate/spiration: a term derived from the Latin *spiro*, to breathe. The Father and the Son breathe forth or *spirate* the Spirit, while the Spirit is breathed forth or *spirated* by the Father and the Son.

Subordinationism/subordinationist: a particular distortion of Christian belief that views the Son and the Spirit as subordinate to the Father, as somehow less fully divine than the Father.

Substance/consubstantial: the term used to define what is common to Father, Son and Spirit. The substance of a thing is what it really is, and is known through correct understanding.

Transcendence/transcendent: a term used to describe God's relationship to creation. It does not mean "remote" but "other than." So God is other than creation, not necessarily remote from creation.

Tritheism/tritheistic: a particular distortion of Christian belief that results in Father, Son and Spirit being separate beings and hence no longer one God.

Unitarianism/unitarian: a particular distortion of Christian belief that denies the divinity of the Son and the Spirit and so rejects trinitarian belief in three Persons in one God.